ook is to

HOLI

A WORLD OF FESTIVALS

HOLI

Dilip Kadodwala

Evans Brothers Limited

Published by Evans Brothers Limited
2A Portman Mansions
Chiltern Street
London W1M 1LE

© copyright Evans Brothers Limited 1997

First published 1997
Reprinted 1997
First published in paperback in 2000

British Library Cataloguing in Publication data.
A catalogue record for this book is available from the
British Library.

Printed in Spain by G.Z. Printek

0 237 52182 2

ACKNOWLEDGEMENTS

Editor: Su Swallow
Design: Neil Sayer
Production: Jenny Mulvanny

For permission to reproduce copyright material, the
author and publishers gratefully acknowledge the fol-
lowing;

cover: John Hatt/Hutchison Library
title page: Alain Evrard/Robert Harding Picture
Library
page 6 John Hatt/Hutchison Library page 7 (top left)
Trip/H Rogers, (centre) Wanda Warming/Image
Bank, (bottom) Circa Photo Library page 8 (top)
Jaime Villaseca/Image Bank, (bottom) Circa Photo
Library page 9 (top) Robert Harding Picture Library,
(bottom) R. Berriedale-Johnson/Panos Pictures page
10 (top) India Pix/Zul Picture Library, (bottom)
Bipin J. Mistry/Circa Photo Library page 11 (top) J.
Highet, Hutchison Library, (bottom) Circa Photo
Library/John Smith page 12 Jimmy Holmes/Panos
Pictures page 13 (top) Circa Photo Library/John
Smith, (bottom) Trip/Dinodia page 14 National
Museum of India, New Delhi/Bridgeman Art Library
page 15 (top) D Rose, (bottom) Bipin J Mistry page
16 Circa Photo Library/B. J. Mistry page 17 Victoria
and Albert Museum/Bridgeman Art Library page 18
(top) Trip/H Rogers, (bottom) Victoria and Albert
Museum/Bridgeman Art Library page 19 (top) Circa
Photo Library/R. Beeche, (bottom) Trip/H Rogers
page 20 (top left) Trip/H Rogers, (bottom right)
Bipinchandra J Mistry page 21 (top) Bipinchandra J
Mistry, (bottom) Trip/H Rogers page 22 (left) John
Hatt/Hutchison Library, (right) Circa Photo Library
page 23 Alain Evrard/Robert Harding Picture Library
page 24 D Rose page 25 (top) D Rose, (bottom)
Trip/N Ray page 26 Trip/H Rogers page 27 (top)
Tony Gervis/Robert Harding Picture Library,
(bottom) Trip/Dinodia page 28/29 Alan Towse
Photography

Contents

Holi and Hinduism

HOLI IS A HINDU FESTIVAL. Hinduism began in India and is one of the world's oldest religions. It is different from other religions such as Islam and Christianity because it does not have one main person who started it. Hindus may worship one god, many gods or none at all.

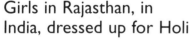
Girls in Rajasthan, in India, dressed up for Holi

THE TREE OF HINDUISM

One way to understand Hinduism is to think of a very old tree. This tree has many roots and branches - and it is still growing! Hinduism has many different beliefs, stories and customs, and it too is still growing and changing.

◄ The banyan tree, like Hinduism, is very ancient. It has roots that grow down from the top into the ground!

Mostly, Hindus believe that God is everywhere and in everything. They call this god Brahman. They believe that this one god – Brahman – can be pictured and thought about in many different forms. These forms are represented by gods and goddesses. The three main gods are Brahma, Vishnu and Shiva. Many Hindu festivals are linked to some of these gods and goddesses. The festival of Holi has exciting stories about Vishnu and some of the other gods.

A colourful image of the god Krishna on a temple wall. There are many stories about Krishna and the Holi festival (see page 18).

◄ Hindu prayers begin and end with the word *om*, which is the symbol for Brahman. This is how it is written in the old Indian language of Sanskrit.

Calendars, colours and crops

Holi begins on a full moon night in spring.

THE FESTIVAL OF HOLI marks the end of winter and the coming of spring. In India, it can last for a week or more, but outside India the celebrations may only last a day or two.

MOON MONTHS

The Hindu calendar is based on the movement of the moon. The calendar has twelve lunar months. Each month is divided into a 'bright half' (from the new moon to the full moon) and a 'dark half' (from the full moon to the next new moon). The lunar months are shorter than the twelve months of our calendar, so the dates of any festival change from year to year. Holi begins on the full moon night of the month of Phalguna (March or early April).

CELEBRATING IN STYLE

Holi is celebrated in different ways in different parts of the world. But Hindus everywhere enjoy bonfires, street processions, music and dancing. Sometimes the festival is called the 'festival of colours', because people spray each other with coloured water. Holi is a festival of fun!

A Hindu calendar with a picture of the god Ganesh

8

At Holi, people look forward to a good harvest

GIVING THANKS

Most people in India live in villages or small towns. For many, growing crops is an important part of their lives. Holi gives Hindus a chance to thank the gods for the harvest to come.

Hindu men and women worshipping at a street shrine. Festivals are special times for worshipping.

Flames and fire, signs and symbols

FIRE AND LIGHT are important to Hindus. They have a special meaning in worship and at festival time, at home and in the temple.

A *diva*, a symbol of God's goodness

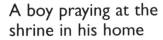
A boy praying at the shrine in his home

LIGHTING THE LAMP

When Hindus worship it is called *puja*. At home, a special place is set aside for *puja*, called a shrine. Hindus also worship at the temple. In either place, worshippers light a small lamp called a *diva*. A *diva* is made of twisted cotton dipped in melted butter. The light of the *diva* is a symbol of God's goodness.

The light is also a symbol of fire, which is one of the five elements of nature. (The others are earth, water, air and space.) All the elements of nature are important to Hindus, for they support life on earth.

A NEW BEGINNING

Hindus believe that fire has the power to purify and cleanse. They worship the god of fire, Agni. For farmers, fire is also important because

A farmer burns the stubble before
planting a new crop.

it helps to renew the land so that crops can grow
afresh. So it is not surprising that the spring
festival of Holi is celebrated by the burning of
fires. Farming communities all over the world
mark the end of winter darkness and welcome
the joy of spring, looking forward to new life.
During Holi, Hindus feel a close link with the
earth, and celebrate the new season with bonfires
and prayers.

Trays of offerings to the bonfire at Holi

The Holi bonfire

O N THE FIRST NIGHT of Holi, the night of the full moon, everyone gathers round a huge bonfire. During the week before, people in villages, towns and cities decide where the main bonfire is to be lit. Then they collect wood for the fire. In fact, anything made of wood is likely to find its way on to the giant heap!

A coconut and garland, offerings for a god in a temple. Coconuts have a special place in the Holi celebrations.

LIGHTING THE BONFIRE
Some Hindus fast on the day before the night of the full moon. As dusk falls, people gather round the bonfire. They bring with them offerings of coconuts, wheat and other grains, which are later thrown into the fire. As the sun sets, a priest says a prayer before lighting the fire.

It is not long before the wood is ablaze!

As the fire burns, the sounds of drums, horns and singing fill the air. In the part of India called Gujarat, parents walk around the fire once with their children. This is a way of receiving the blessings of God for their children. They say prayers for the children's good health and happiness. Gujarati Hindus in other parts of the world celebrate Holi in the same way.

COOKING COCONUTS

Coconuts are a symbol of new life. Coconuts that have been thrown into the fire are shared out between the worshippers - they are ready to eat when the outer shell is charred. The white nut on the inside tastes good! It is called *prashad*, food blessed by God.

FOOD FROM THE GROUND

Some people light small fires outside their own homes. In Gujarat, people dig a hole and bury wheat in a clay pot. The hole is covered with earth and the Holi fire is built on top. When the fire dies out, the pot is pulled out. The next day, everyone shares a meal of the cooked wheat.

Women place offerings of popcorn, fruit and coconuts round the Holi bonfire.

Dancing round the ashes of a Holi bonfire

The power of good over evil

MANY STORIES are told at Holi. Sometimes they are acted out for people to watch. Whatever the story, one message is at the heart of them all: good always triumphs over evil.

THE STORY OF PRAHLAD

A popular Holi story is about a prince called Prahlad. He lived with his father, King Hiranyakashipu, and the king's sister, Holika. The king spent many hours praying. As he was so devoted to God, he was granted a special wish by God. The king wished that he would never die. God granted that he would not die during the day or night, he would not be killed by a human or an animal or any weapon, and he would not die inside or outside a house.

The king stopped worshipping God and ordered his people to worship him instead. But Prince Prahlad refused. The king became very angry and forced his son into a pit of poisonous snakes. Prahlad prayed to the god Vishnu for help, and he was saved. This made the king even angrier. He ordered an elephant to charge at Prahlad. Prahlad

A stone statue of Vishnu, the god who protected Prahlad

14

prayed to Vishnu, and the elephant stopped and bowed down in front of him.

By now the king was mad with rage. His sister Holika decided to help him. She had a special cloth which protected her against fire. She made Prahlad go into a huge bonfire with her. Prahlad prayed to Vishnu, and walked out of the fire unharmed! But Holika died.

Building fires at Holi is a reminder to Hindus of Prahlad's faith in God and God's power to defeat evil.

The red and yellow cloth in the Holi bonfire is a symbol of the cloth that protected Holika against fire.

Prahlad and Holika, who went into a huge bonfire together

15

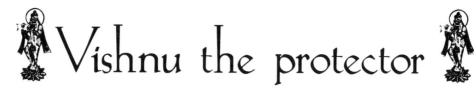

Vishnu the protector

ANOTHER HOLI STORY tells how Vishnu defeated the wicked King Hirayanakashipu(see page 14). It happened when the wicked king ordered his son Prahlad to hug a red-hot iron pillar.

A PILLAR OF STRENGTH

Prahlad prayed to Vishnu to protect him. Then he noticed a line of ants moving unharmed up the hot pillar. This was a sign that the pillar would not harm Prahlad. So Prahlad hugged the pillar.

As he did so, thunder and lightning raged across the sky. The pillar burst open and there stood the god Vishnu! He was half lion, half human. In one stride he reached the king as he stood in the palace doorway, and tore him apart!

People remembered that God had promised the king that he would not die during the day or night, would not be killed by a human or an animal, or a weapon, inside or outside a house. So, why and how did the king die?

Vishnu appeared as the sun was setting, so it was neither day nor night. Vishnu appeared as neither human or animal, but both. The king died with one foot in the palace and the other outside so he was neither inside or outside. And lastly the King was killed by the lion's sharp claws, and not by any weapons! Once again, goodness had triumphed over evil.

The god Vishnu is often shown with a conch shell. This man blows a conch to help him concentrate on prayer and to let Vishnu know that he is ready to worship.

These pictures show Vishnu in some of his different forms. Can you see him with a lion's head?

17

Playing tricks

A T HOLI, many Hindus start the day of the bonfire by visiting the temple to worship. What happens later depends on where you are - every part of India has its own way of enjoying the fun of Holi.

Holi may begin on a serious note, with a visit to the temple.

This painting was made 200 years ago. It shows the god Krishna and some women enjoying colour fights at Holi.

KRISHNA AND HIS COLOURS

Krishna is another god who has special links with Holi. In fact, Krishna is one of the forms taken by Vishnu when he visits Earth. There are many stories about Krishna's childhood and his adventures as a young man.

Krishna is a handsome god who plays such beautiful tunes on his flute that people rush to worship him (see page 7). When he was young he liked playing tricks on people. He even played tricks on someone he loved - the beautiful Princess Radha. Once he threw coloured powders over Radha. Since that time, people celebrate Holi by throwing coloured powder and water on one another.

Some of the colours for Holi are made from flowers which are soaked in water overnight. Others are made by using coloured powders mixed in water. Red, yellow and blue are mixed together to make different colours.

FAMILY FUN

People like to play other tricks at Holi, too. It is often the women in the family who get up to mischief. A wife might hide her husband's shoes, a little girl might jump out and frighten her father, or leave a bag of coloured powder hidden ready to fall on someone's head! For Hindus, playing tricks and jokes is not only fun, it is a reminder of God's playful nature.

Two children dressed as Krishna, ready to squirt their canisters of coloured water

Coloured powders for sale for Holi

Colour, colour everywhere!

No MATTER WHERE YOU ARE, throwing coloured water is always part of Holi. In some parts of India, it happens before the bonfire. In other places it happens afterwards. Everywhere, though, the most important thing is to have fun!

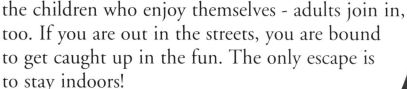

Bottles, bags, balloons and pumps – they are all good for spraying coloured water over other people!

No escape

One way to spray other people is simply to throw buckets of coloured water over them. A good way to surprise people is to fill balloons with coloured water, climb on to a balcony and pop the balloon above the heads of passers-by! Another favourite is to use squirters or pumps full of water. And it's not just the children who enjoy themselves - adults join in, too. If you are out in the streets, you are bound to get caught up in the fun. The only escape is to stay indoors!

A change of clothes

In some places, people stop throwing the coloured water at each other at lunch time. They go home and change out of their wet clothes and

A girl in her best dress, ready to go visiting

A little girl smears colour over her father's face.

into their best clothes. But the fun is not over yet - now it is time to smear dry colours over each other!

Later, in the evening, families and friends visit each other, taking presents of sweets with them.

A dish of Indian sweets fit for any festival

Holi hai! Holi hai!

'HOLI HAI!' (Holi is here!) is the cry that can be heard above the beating of the drums, as people dance and spray colours. One way to celebrate is to hold mock fights.

Women dancing at Holi

BAMBOO BATTLES

In Mathura, in northern India, men and women stage mock stick fights. It is all done in good fun and reminds people of the tricks Krishna once played on Radha. Men and women face each other in two rows, armed with long bamboo sticks. As they 'fight', supporters of each team attack their opponents with coloured water. As the players are soaked and beaten, they drop out and are

Music in the street adds to the fun of Holi

replaced by 'dry' players. Men who are touched by a woman's bamboo stick are said to receive Radha's blessings for the year to come.

FLOATS AND FRIENDSHIP

Processions of carts and decorated floats wind their way through the streets at Holi. In one place, spectators take great delight in trying to knock strong men off the carts with fast-flowing jets of coloured water. Elsewhere, stories linked with Holi are acted out, and huge statues of Krishna and other gods are paraded through the town. Everyone is caught up in the carnival atmosphere. Neighbours forget their quarrels and friendships are renewed.

Fishing boats in Bombay, with their flags flying for Holi

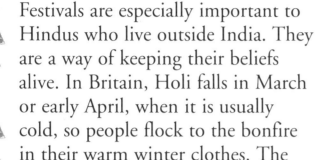 Outside India

MOST HINDUS LIVE IN INDIA, but there are many Hindus living in other parts of the world. How do they celebrate Holi?

COLD CLIMATE

Festivals are especially important to Hindus who live outside India. They are a way of keeping their beliefs alive. In Britain, Holi falls in March or early April, when it is usually cold, so people flock to the bonfire in their warm winter clothes. The wood for the bonfire is collected in a local park. A priest says some prayers and as the sun sets the fire is lit. If the sky is too cloudy to see the sun, the priest decides when to light the fire.

The Holi bonfire roars into flame in a park in Britain.

Prayers and offerings round the bonfire

CELEBRATIONS IN NEPAL

In Britain, Holi lasts for just a day, but in Nepal, where most people are Hindu, Holi lasts for a week! A week before the full moon, a huge pole called a *chir* is put up. On the pole are strips of cloth which are good luck charms. As the pole is put up, the festivities begin. People sing, dance and make merry. At the end of the week, they throw coloured water at each other, and the pole is taken to a bonfire. As it passes, people try to grab a strip of cloth, to bring them good fortune in the year to come.

A Hindu shrine in Nepal

Fairs and feasts

I N SOME PARTS OF INDIA, huge fairs are held at Holi. And everyone celebrates by eating their favourite foods.

A string puppet. Puppet shows are popular at festival times.

ALL THE FUN OF THE FAIR

Holi fairs are held in vast open places. Thousands of people flock to enjoy the festive fun. There are stalls selling snacks and sweets, merry-go-rounds and puppet shows. There is music too - especially drums and wind instruments - and you will probably see some dancing.

FOOD FACTS

Some Hindus, especially mothers of young children, do not eat anything during the day of the Holi full moon. This is a way of asking God to bless their children with good health and happiness. After the bonfire, they break the fast by eating the coconuts cooked in the fire. Later, they enjoy a meal with their family. Other Hindus prefer to eat a feast at mid-day. Outside India, some Hindus like to eat at a restaurant.

Many Hindus are vegetarian. They like to eat vegetable curries, lentils, rice and chappati, a kind of bread. In some parts of the world, especially in India, some Hindus sit cross-legged on the floor to eat. Food can be served in a *thali* - a metal dish covered in small portions of all kinds of foods. The *thali* may have sweets on it, too, called *barfi. Barfi* is made from milk which can be flavoured with nuts - and it tastes really good!

ENDINGS AND BEGINNINGS

For Hindus, Holi is a time for joy and laughter. It is a time to celebrate the bounty of mother earth, a time to thank God and to make peace with friends and neighbours. And Holi would not be the same without jokes and colour splashing!

As Holi ends, Hindus look forward to the next celebration, for the Hindu world is full of rich festivals.

▶ A vegetable market in Delhi, the capital of India

▼ Sitting cross-legged on the floor for a feast!

Let's celebrate!

Join in the fun! Try making this elephant mask (see the story on page 14) and taste a sweet called *barfi* (see page 26).

MAKING AN ELEPHANT MASK

You will need:

1 a cardboard box that fits easily over your head
2 card
3 PVA glue and sticky tape
4 paints and felt-tip pens
5 sequins, sweet wrappers, coloured braid or any other bright decorations
6 safe scissors

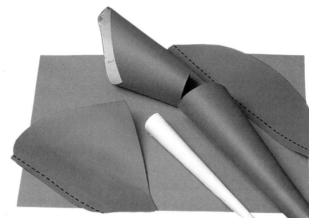

All you have to do is:

1 Cut out these shapes from card:
   a trunk (two square pieces of card curled round, stuck and cut to shape), two ears, the top of the head, two tusks. Use the picture to help you. Remember that Indian elephants have small ears!
2 Paint the box and the pieces in grey, except for the tusks.
3 Draw dotted lines on the ears and the top of the head, as in the picture.
4 Fit the top half of the trunk inside the bottom half and stick them together, making the trunk bend. Then stick the whole thing to the front of the box.
5 Bend back the ears and the top of the head at the dotted lines, and stick them down to the box. Then stick the tusks to the inside of the box.
6 Cut small holes at either side of the trunk, so that you can see through the box.
7 Now paint the eyes and decorate your mask.

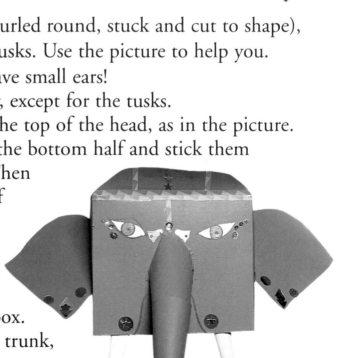

MAKING BARFI

Barfi is a sweet made from milk. It is best to eat it on the day you make it.

ASK AN ADULT TO HELP YOU

You will need:

non-stick pan
wooden spoon
greased baking tray
$\frac{1}{2}$ litre milk
1 kilo granulated sugar
100 grammes of butter
1 kilo dried milk powder
$\frac{1}{2}$ cup dessicated coconut
$\frac{1}{2}$ cup chopped almonds and
   pistachio nuts

All you have to do is:

1 Heat the milk gently in a saucepan. Add the sugar and stir continuously while bringing the mixture to the boil.

2 When the mixture is boiling, add the butter, stirring continuously.

3 When the butter has dissolved, add the chopped almonds, nuts and coconut.

4 Remove the mixture from the heat and add the dried milk powder. Stir thoroughly.

5 Pour the mixture out on to a lightly greased baking tray and spread evenly.

6 Wait for the mixture to cool down. This could take up to 4 hours.

7 When cooled, cut the mixture into squares or diamond shapes.

8 Eat some and share them with friends!

Glossary

chir a large pole decorated with strips of cloth

diva a lamp light made out of twisted cotton wool which is dipped in melted butter

fast to eat only certain foods or nothing at all

lentils one of the oldest crops grown all over the Middle East and India; the seeds are green or brown

prashad food such as fruit and nuts which is offered to the gods

puja a time of Hindu worship during which offerings of light and prayers are made

Om (also spelt Aum) a sacred Hindu word for God

thali a round tray used for serving food

vegetarian a person who does not eat meat or fish

Index